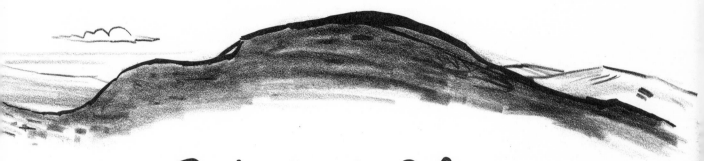

Enchantment of America
NEVADA

FROM ITS GLORIOUS PAST TO THE PRESENT

By Allan Carpenter

Illustrations by Roger Herrington

CHILDRENS PRESS, Chicago

For their advice, counsel and gracious help, the author thanks:

Nevada Historical Society
Clara S. Beatty, Director, Nevada Historical Society
Nevada Department of Economic Development
F. W. Millard
White Pine Public Museum, Inc.
Storey County Commissioners
Las Vegas Chamber of Commerce
Nevada State Park System
Reno Chamber of Commerce

Contents

A True Story to Set the Scene

Poet of the Willow Twigs

She was born in Nevada before white men were ever known there. She grew up without any formal education or other "advantages." She lived all of her ninety-six years in a remote and at first uncivilized land. Many people might have called her a simple savage, reared among a tribe of savages.

And yet she gained an international reputation — has even been called one of the great artists of the world. Experts say her work is perhaps the finest ever done in her art in the history of mankind.

Those who believe that only the most highly educated people or that only those with the whitest skins can do worthwhile things in art would find it hard to explain the amazing story of one of Nevada's most famous women — the Washoe Indian, Dat-So-La-Lee.

For nearly a century, Dat-So-La-Lee labored in the art for which her small tribe has become best-known — the art of basket weaving.

During her life, this cranky old woman made a total of 256 baskets. So beautiful and skillful was her work that this must be considered as one of the great artistic achievements. Her only tools were her teeth, her finger nails, and sometimes a piece of broken glass.

Dat-So-La-Lee found and cut all her own basket-making materials. She sought the straightest twigs of the willows growing near the streams. In early spring she gathered the roots of the black mountain fern and in summer those of the redbud, and these materials gave the color to her designs.

Only after her materials had dried and cured for at least a year did she consider them ready for use.

The shape and designs for her baskets she took from the life and traditions of her Washoe people. Each basket was given a name appropriate to its pattern and design. An authority on baskets, Myrtle Tate Myles, called her a poet as well as an artist, because her baskets tell a story or record the history of her tribe in the most poetical terms.

An example of this is her design which the basket-maker called "When the Fledgling Birds Leave Their Nests and Fly Away, the Indians Will Move to New Homes." This wonderful basket took six months to make and contains 50,000 stitches.

Another basket was given the poetic title "Myriads of Stars Shine Over the Graves of My Ancestors."

In her later life, Dat-So-La-Lee made her home with a Carson City couple, Mr. and Mrs. Abe Cohn. She worked there in winter and at Lake Tahoe during the summer.

Some of her finest baskets took more than a year to make. She is said to be the only basketmaker whose work ever showed absolutely true perspective. Myrtle Myles called her baskets "Marvels of symmetry and grace." She added, "Her baskets rise from the base in absolutely true proportion." Dat-So-La-Lee had the understanding and patience to work with infinite care and skill.

She was born in about the year 1829. In 1925, in her ninety-sixth year, she was still hard at work on one of her most beautiful baskets when she died.

Many wanted to buy this last unfinished masterpiece, which she called "Friendship." But according to the ancient customs of the Washoes, this basket must be buried with her. According to her last wish Friendship followed her to her grave at Carson City.

In all her years, Dat-So-La-Lee never duplicated a design, as this would have been contrary to the customs of her tribe, and so each basket called for a new and fresh idea.

Examples of her work are cherished in fine museums all over the world. The Smithsonian Institution in Washington has some of Dat-So-La-Lee's best work.

Her finest basket, called "Migration" was sold for $10,000.00.

And so the story of how one of Nevada's native daughters found her own way to fame through her skill and patience becomes another of the many fascinating true accounts of the enchantment of Nevada.

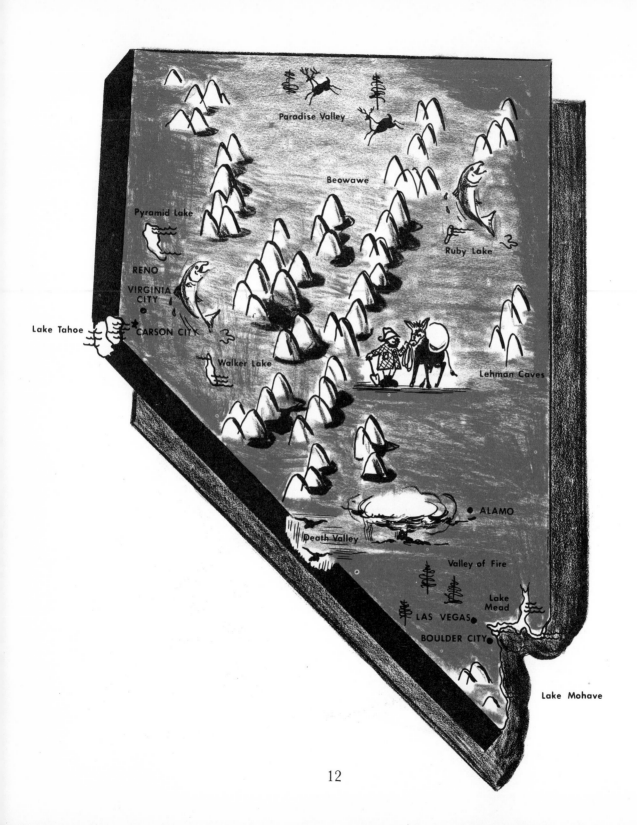

Paradise Valley

Beowawe

Pyramid Lake

Ruby Lake

RENO

VIRGINIA
CITY

Lake Tahoe

CARSON CITY

Walker Lake

Lehman Caves

ALAMO

Death Valley

Valley of Fire

Lake
Mead

LAS VEGAS

BOULDER CITY

Lake Mohave

12

Lay of the Land

When kings of old became very wealthy, they often built strong buildings to hold their treasures, and the kings' guards protected this wealth with their lives.

Nature built a secure place of this kind in America, filling it with unbelievable amounts of gold and silver and precious jewels. The treasure house was so well guarded by parching deserts and rugged mountains that its doors have only been opened for a little more than a hundred years.

This treasure house is Nevada, where wealth has been laid up in the earth for more millions of years than anyone can determine.

All natural forces have been violently at work in this region. Several times the land sank under shallow seas, only to rise again above the surface. During this period, plants and sea animals grew and were swallowed up over and over again, creating mineral deposits of various kinds. Searing heat, the bitter cold of glaciers, pressure and chemical changes all worked to produce and bring together one of the greatest and most varied collections of useful minerals found anywhere in such a comparatively small area.

The region we now call Nevada lies in what is known as the Great Basin. Actually this is no longer really a "basin." Over the centuries, silt, pouring down from ancient mountain ranges on either side, has filled in the basin, making it in reality a high plateau.

Today, the portion of the plateau occupied by Nevada is dotted with mountain ranges. Much of this state, the 7th in size of all our states, is forbidding, dry country, relieved here and there by lakes, river valleys and green highlands. Boundary Peak, on the line between California and Nevada rises to 13,145 feet.

In ancient times, huge lakes occupied much of Nevada. Before recorded time, Bonneville Lake covered much of Utah and extended into eastern Nevada. Prehistoric Lake Lahontan was 250 miles long and 180 miles wide — about the size of present day Lake Erie, but much deeper. Several smaller lakes still remain as fragments of Lake Lahontan. These include Walker and Pyramid lakes.

Pyramid Lake is still the largest lake within the state, about thirty miles long and seven miles wide. Many people have felt that Pyramid

13

Lake is similar to the Biblical Sea of Galilee, because of its appearance and surroundings.

The name of Pyramid Lake comes from rock islands jutting above its surface roughly in pyramid form. One of these islands towers to almost 500 feet above the water. Hot springs on this pyramid puff out wisps of steam, giving an awesome effect. The Indians say the pyramid is a basket used to smother a wicked squaw, and the steam is her breath coming through the cracks of the basket.

Beautiful Lake Tahoe, shared by Nevada and California, is one of the most famous in the world.

In addition to these and other natural lakes, Nevada shares the world's greatest artificial lake with Arizona and Utah. This is Lake Mead, formed by waters of the Colorado River backing up behind Hoover Dam, holding the largest volume of water of any man-made lake. Lahontan and Rye Patch reservoirs are other lakes formed by the damming of rivers.

The Colorado River flows south of Hoover Dam to form the southeast border of Nevada. The Humboldt River is the longest within the state, and another well-known river is the Truckee, which ends in Pyramid Lake. Many of Nevada's rivers, including the Humboldt, flow into desert sinks, to expire there without a further trace.

Mysterious Amargosa River flows most of its course underground, reappearing occasionally to flow for a time on the surface only to disappear again.

The forces of Nature continue to be active in Nevada. Near Frenchman is an area where the earth is settling more rapidly on one side of a line than on the other, sometimes causing sharp earthquakes. This line is called a "fault" and the Nevada fault is considered to be one of the "most spectacular faults in the world."

Water and steam bubble and burst forth from the earth's surface in the Beowawe geyser basin, this country's largest active geyser field outside Yellowstone Park. Other hot springs are found in many parts of Nevada.

Weird traces of volcanic forces at work in Nevada not more than 1,000 years ago are found in the lava rock formations of lunar crater, the dead remains of a violent explosion of the earth which threw chunks the size of city blocks high into the air.

Collecting Your Thoughts

What do you feel is the single most important gift of Nature to Nevada? Why?

Is it likely that many valuable resources are still undiscovered in the state?

15

Footsteps on the Land

Giving Tongues to the Dead

Near Tule Springs a man chewed on a large bone and tossed it carelessly away. This hardly seems like an event to be recorded in history, but the human toothmarks on that bone tell us that human beings have lived in Nevada for at least 23,800 years.

Many thousands of other items left behind by ancient peoples in Nevada help to show who they were, how long ago they lived and the manner of their lives.

More than 10,000 separate relics of ancient peoples have been brought from Lovelock Caves. In this part of Nevada the climate is said to be better than that of ancient Egypt for preserving relics over the centuries.

As in Egypt, many mummies have been found in Nevada Caves. In the years before the scientific value of these relics was generally known, one of the finest of these mummies was boiled by a Nevada fraternal group in order to get the skeleton for initiation rites.

Among the particularly interesting relics found in Lovelock Caves were the duck decoys of ancient hunters, carefully painted and feathered by hands dead many thousands of years.

Discovery of 16½-inch long moccasins used by these Sai-i people caused some experts to wonder if these particular ancient men and women may have been a race of giants.

Over the years, the ancient peoples of Nevada improved their condition. We know that they mined salt. Some of them were able to grow crops using rather elaborate systems of irrigation. Some of these ancient irrigation canals can still be traced, and the storehouses show evidence of the beans, corn, cotton and squash that once were kept in them.

They learned how to weave baskets and later developed a method of making decorated glazed pottery, and wove cotton cloth, all this before the birth of Christ.

Most of the very early Nevadans were nomads who did not build permanent cities, but at least one city was built and occupied in Nevada for a very long time. This has been named Pueblo Grande de Nevada. After it disappeared under the rising waters of Lake Mead,

Pueblo Grande became known by the popular name of "Lost City."

Carved camel heads, polished bobbins, woven fabrics and dozens of other kinds of objects have all been found and preserved, many in the State Historical Museum at Reno. Atlatls have been found proving that Nevada's early people knew how to use this kind of throwing weapon which preceded the bow and arrow.

Other important archeological discoveries have been made in Lehman Caves, Gypsum Cave and Tule Springs.

Dr. Mark Harrington of the Southwest Museum has been the principal discoverer of ancient relics in Nevada.

17

Makers of War and Baskets

Although the region was bleak, there may have been more Indians in Nevada at the time the white man came than there were in much more agreeable locations to the east. Arrowheads are found throughout the state, and a number of tribes coaxed a living from the arid land.

Most Nevada Indians are of the Shoshonian group, which includes Utes, Paiutes and Goshutes, and Shoshone. The region of Lake Tahoe was home to a small tribe called Wasau (or Washoe). They were not related to any other Indian groups, and they had a world-wide reputation as basketmakers. Dot-So-La-Lee was a member of this tribe.

Indians of Nevada wore blankets woven from strips of field mice, rabbits and coyote fur. They dried and smoked the curious cui-cui fish of Pyramid Lake. They hunted for game, no matter how small or insignificant. They worked the turquoise mines in Clark County, and it is thought that some of the finest Nevada turquoise may have found their way to far off Mexico, skillfully worked into the jewelry of the Mayas and Aztecs.

As the white men came into their territory, the Indians became more and more restless. The whites stripped the land of the piñon trees on which Indians depended for food. In revenge the Indians attacked many immigrant parties, killing their people or driving off their livestock, or robbing them of all they had.

But the Indians could not withstand the white man, and today they live quietly on reservations.

One of the most famous of Nevada Indians was Chief Winnemucca, for whom the Nevada town is named. An interesting story is told of the meeting between Chief Winnemucca and Governor Nye, an early Nevada leader. Nye went to Winnemucca's camp on the Truckee River near Pyramid Lake. Winnemucca came to the conference in a kingly manner, attended by 400 warriors. They tried to impress the governor with their bravery by keeping up a war dance during the meetings, sometimes on live coals. No treaties were made, but both sides became more friendly.

Only A Few

The exact history of white exploration in Nevada is not known. Father Escalante, a Spanish Priest, and his party are said to have visited Nevada in 1775, and Father Francisco Tomás Garcés is also supposed to have been there, but proof of these claims is lacking.

The earliest white man of record in Nevada did not come until 1826. This was Peter Skene Ogden, who was exploring for the Hudson's Bay Company. Another fur scout, Jedediah Smith, also crossed what is now southern Nevada completely and then re-crossed it in central Nevada on his return.

Other traders came to Nevada country during the late 1820's.

In the years 1829 to 1830 American and Mexican parties blazed a route across southern Nevada which has come to be known as the "Old Spanish Trail."

Joseph Walker led an expedition over Nevada in 1833, down the Humboldt River and into California. The pass across the mountains which they used is now called Walker pass. Walker Lake was first seen by this man whose name it bears.

The first really complete reports on Nevada came after the explorations of John C. Fremont, with his famous guide Kit Carson. Fremont, Carson and Walker, traveled in Nevada during 1843-1844, discovering Pyramid Lake.

Parties of settlers headed for California had begun to pass through Nevada as early as 1841, when the Bidwell-Bartleson group made the difficult journey.

On the way to their tragic fate in the Sierra snows, the Donner party made their way across Nevada in 1846 and lingered there just a day too long to escape the snows.

At this time, Nevada was still part of the vast territories claimed first by Spain and later by Mexico. But the Nevada portion was almost totally ignored by Spain and Mexico. The region which is now Nevada was turned over to the United States at the end of the war with Mexico.

Just at the time this occurred, another event took place which was to change the West for all time. The discovery of gold in California seemed to send the whole world charging toward that promised land of fortune. Those who came overland must necessarily cross Nevada, much as they might have wished to avoid such a journey. There began an almost endless crossing of the state by people who hoped to make their fortunes in California.

On foot, by mule back, on horseback, or in covered wagons, they came in ever increasing numbers, making the difficult, sometimes desperate journey along the overland trails.

Nevada's forty-mile desert was the worst. When the travelers staggered to the Carson River where Fallon now is, after forty miles of the most awful passage through choking clouds of alkali dust, the flowing waters of the river seemed like paradise.

The industrious Mormons came to the Carson Valley in 1849 to establish a trading post and help attend to the needs of the travelers. Mormon Station was begun in 1851, and was the first permanent settlement in Nevada. Later the name was changed to Genoa.

In 1850 the Territory of Utah was formed, including present-day Nevada, and the noted Mormon leader, Brigham Young, served as Governor of this great territory from 1850 to 1858, with headquarters at Salt Lake City.

By the fall of 1850, the incredible number of 60,000 persons had scrambled up the Carson River on the way to California.

Gradually, the Mormon settlers spread into other Nevada regions, Genoa, Mottsville and Pioche.

Another of these was Big Meadows, where the travelers paused for rest and repairs to their equipment before making the mad dash across the dread 40-mile desert. Big Meadows was the site of present-day Lovelock.

Carson County was established in 1851, with flourishing Genoa as its County Seat.

Bonanza!

Some of the hurrying travelers had actually discovered gold as early as 1847. Because of this discovery, the location was named Gold Canyon. It was at the foot of Mount Davidson in the region called Washoe by the Indians. But most of the immigrants hurried on without stopping there.

However, a few tried their luck with great success. One lucky searcher is reported to have dug out $30,000 worth of gold in a summer, while another said he scrounged out gold dust worth over $7,000 — in a single day!

There was no great rush to Gold Canyon during the period after gold was first found, but men like Sandy Bowers and desert herder Henry Thomas Paige Comstock stopped there. Some of those who had gone on to California returned to try their luck at Gold Canyon. Some of these had been in the California gold fields — some successful, others not; now they were trying their hand in what later became Nevada.

About this time one of the most famous women of the west came into the region. This was Eilley Orrum, who set up a boarding house in a camp called Johntown.

All of these people were soon to take a prominent place in the history of Nevada.

Gradually a crowd of gold seekers spread farther and farther up the slope of Mount Davidson searching for the wealth of Gold Canyon. Many of these were desperate men, thieves and murderers, who had been run out of more "settled" areas in California.

In unorganized "Utah Territory" they found the lack of law and order much to their liking. Gambling, claim jumping, murder all went on almost unnoticed.

However, in the spring of 1851, there had come to Gold Canyon two young men who were completely unlike most of the others. These were the Grosch Brothers, Hosea and Allen. They were the well educated sons of a prominent eastern preacher. The Grosch boys ventured into Nevada to make their fortunes in order to help their father.

Before long, they found that their gold-bearing ore was clogged with "that blue stuff." All the miners complained about that awful blue clay. It clung to the gold so firmly that the precious metal was difficult to remove, and the blue stuff greatly reduced the quantity of the gold. The miners threw it away with curses, and would have given anything to be rid of the stuff.

But the Grosch Brothers had inquiring minds. They felt that at least they should try to find out exactly what the "blue stuff" was, and they had the knowledge and ability to make the necessary tests.

When they saw the results of their tests they could hardly believe their good fortune. That despised and hated blue stuff was almost pure silver!

Only they knew the great secret of the Washoe country and of Mount Davidson, and only they would ever know it if the Grosch boys had their way.

They prospected farther and farther up the slopes, but now they were looking for silver and gold, not gold alone. Going farther than anyone had before, at last they discovered a spot where the blue was bluer and the gold specks in it more sparkling than anywhere else.

Later they took out enough of the silver ore for an assay, which showed that it might be worth three to four thousand dollars per ton. But they had no money to set up large scale mining operations, and they were afraid to let more than one partner into their secret. Then Hosea injured himself with a pick. He died shortly afterward of what appeared to be lockjaw.

Allen Grosch decided to go to California with complete proof of their claims and try to raise money. He asked H. T. P. Comstock to look after the Grosch cabin during the winter and gave him an agreement for a fourth interest in their claims for his services. But Allen Grosch refused to tell either his helper, Richard Bucke or Comstock exactly where the claims were, nor did he ever reveal the value of the blue clay.

Then Grosch and Bucke started over the Sierra Nevadas. By this time it was November, 1857, and the winter was much too far advanced for any trip over the Sierra Nevadas.

Their trip was a nightmare. The last day, half frozen, they crawled on hands and knees. The precious packet describing the Grosch claims had been left behind in the snow. They were rescued by miners and taken to a mining camp, but Allen Grosch lay in delirium for a time and at last died from the results of his awful exposure. Bucke recovered after a long illness, and later became one of Canada's most famous doctors. In later years he placed a monument at the roadside grave of Allen Grosch, but he never discovered the Groschs' secret.

And so the secret of the wealth of Gold Canyon died for a time with the two fine young men who bore the first of a flood of heartbreak and tragedy which was to be connected with their discovery, along with some of the most exciting pages of American history.

Most of the Johntown miners cared nothing for the Grosch brothers. Comstock, however, knew there must be wealth in the region if he could only rediscover it. He wandered over the mountainside, locating claims at every likely spot. He and other prospectors did find some rich veins, but they continued to look for gold and ignore the wealth of silver they were throwing away.

The story is told that in 1859 or 60 a group of miners who had celebrated a little too much were wandering about the area when one of them fell with a bottle of whiskey in his hand. This was James Fennimore, who was called "Old Virginny" because he came from Virginia. As he fell Virginny smashed the whiskey bottle against the rock accidentally. Not wanting to waste the whiskey, he called out, "Virginia Town, I baptize thee."

This, according to the story, is the way that Virginia City got its name.

Virginia City and the whole region around were becoming famous for gold, and Comstock, Old Virginny and the rest were working their claims and still cursing the blue stuff which kept them from getting at the gold as readily as they would have liked.

Then in 1859, a visitor to Virginia City took away some samples of the blue clay; the samples found their way to Melville Atwood's assay office. Atwood found that the ore was worth almost $5,000 per ton in gold and silver, the larger part of it in almost solid silver.

Before long the secret was out, and the incredible flood of prospectors started toward the Washoe region. Most of those who went were prospectors who had come to California in the gold rush there. Now they were after the silver of Nevada. For a time it appeared that the whole population of California was on its way to the fields of silver and gold.

Because of Comstock's loud bragging and his many claims, the whole region soon became known as "The Comstock," but Comstock himself sold out for relatively little, as did many of the other pioneers on the Comstock lode.

There were no accommodations waiting for prospectors when they arrived. Many of them burrowed into the hillside. The only available drinking water was so full of minerals it made them sick. The whole countryside had been completely stripped of piñon pine, the only growing things.

During the winter of 1859-1860, supplies in the Virginia City area almost gave out. What little flour was still available was selling at $85 per sack. Everything, of course, had to be brought over the mountains at great expense.

After the worst of the winter, when the first load of flour could get into Virginia City, the men were so hungry they mixed it with snow and ate the batter raw.

Soon, loads of precious ore were being shipped by mule train over the mountains to California for processing. Back over those same mountains came all the things needed to support life in Virginia City, Gold Hill and Silver City and the whole mushrooming community on Mount Davidson.

Before long, mills were set up along the Carson River to refine the ore, using the Washoe Process of Pan Amalgamation, developed by a local man, Almarin Paul. The great mill hammers crushed the ore for treatment in huge iron pans, and the sound resounded through the canyons.

More water was needed and timber in tremendous quantities. Timber was used to hold up the roofs of the mine tunnels and it was burned in the mills. All the piñon trees on which the Indians so long had depended for food had been cut for fuel. There was no timber nearby.

Finally, in a great engineering feat, a flume and pipeline were built clear from Marlette Lake to bring the waters of the lake to the Comstock and other flumes were built to carry timbers from the shores of Lake Tahoe to Washoe Valley saw mills.

Within a short time, the breathtaking eastern shores of Lake Tahoe had been stripped of their beauty to feed the "monster of Washoe" with virgin timber.

And still the treasure seekers came to the Comstock, streaming up Gold Canyon. Permanent buildings sprang up in Virginia City. By 1863 the business section of Virginia City had taken on a metropolitan look. The Pioneer Stage Company ran twelve giant Concord coaches through Virginia City, now, unbelievably a city of 25,000 people. All of Gold Canyon had become one continuous "civilization," crowded with mills, water wheels, houses, sluices, tunnels and dumps.

The mules, called "Washoe Canaries" by the miners, were not strong enough nor fast enough for some, and camels were imported from Arabia. Visitors were startled to see camel caravans plodding through the Nevada deserts, each beast carrying 800 pounds of salt to Austin and Virginia City. Horses bolted when they caught sight of these awful "monsters."

Where only short months before travelers had struggled hazardously through rugged mountain passes, over this route now flowed the wealth of the Comstock and the luxuries for Virginia City and its neighbors.

Strange as it now seems, Virginia City had become the second most important city in the West, only a little behind San Francisco. It

boasted four banks, six churches, even an opera house, and had the only elevator between San Francisco and Chicago. Most unbelievably of all, however, it supported 110 saloons and gambling houses. Some of them had mahogany or ebony bars, many inlaid with intricate ivory or brass patterns. Over some of the more elegant bars, were murals painted by some of the best-known artists of the day, imported for the purpose at great expense.

The streets of Virginia City had to be seen to be believed. Many lavish and wonderful homes had been built along the alkaline choked avenues. Six-horse stages, mule trains, Wells Fargo express wagons, horsemen — all pushed through clouds of dust which obscured garish posters of theaters and saloons, and dozens of Indians.

All this had sprung up in the course of less than four years on a completely desolate and barren mountainside, as if conjured over-night by some powerful genii.

Incredible fortunes were made and lost in this mad rush for wealth at the Comstock. More will be said about this in a later section.

As the Comstock grew, the need for government and all the other necessities of civilization grew with it.

The Paiutes rebelled against the treatment of the whites and the loss of their lands and food supplies. The short but bitter Paiute War in the spring of 1860 cost several lives, including that of Henry Meredith and Captain Edward F. Storey, for whom Storey County, Nevada, is named.

To protect the white settlers, Fort Churchill had been established in 1860.

In 1861 the Territory of Nevada was created. President Abraham Lincoln appointed his friend James W. Nye to be first Governor of the territory. This wildest of the wild west must have seemed strange to Nye, a New York City man, but he took it in his stride.

Nevada — War-Time Savior

Nevada was far away from the center of the dispute over slavery which had been tearing the country apart, but when Civil War came to the United States, it was to bring Governor Nye one of his greatest problems.

At the beginning of the war, there were many southern sympathizers in the Nevada area. In fact, it appeared that the Southerners might be able to take control in Nevada. If the Confederacy could have gained the wealth of the Comstock, the whole outcome of the Civil War might have been changed.

As it was, the forces in Nevada which were loyal to the Union, with the help of Governor Nye, were able to keep the territory on the side of the Union.

During the Civil War, the Territory of Nevada and the state of California fought a little "war" all their own; the dispute was called the Sagebrush War. Both California and Nevada claimed territory in the Sierra country, and the boundary had never been completely settled. Tempers ran high in the area; "armies" of posses were formed on both sides, and it looked as if a real battle might take place.

But calmer thinking won out just in time, and a commission was appointed to settle the dispute. The decision of the Commission went in California's favor.

As the Civil War raged on, however, most other matters were going in Nevada's favor.

It is a strange and little-known fact of United States history that to a large extent the wealth of the Comstock kept the government of the country solvent in spite of its huge wartime expenses. No less an authority than President Lincoln asserted, ". . . the gold and silver in the region . . . has made it possible for the government to maintain sufficient credit to continue this terrible war for the Union."

By an accident of history, one of the greatest discoveries of mineral wealth came about at the exact time the nation so desperately needed it for survival.

While their silver was supporting the war effort, the people of the Comstock were enjoying their prosperity. A branch of the U.S. mint was established at Carson City. The Superintendent of the Gould and Curry mine received a yearly salary of $40,000.00, much larger than that of the President of the United States, and one of the largest salaries paid anywhere in the country. The greatest stars of stage and opera were presented at Virginia City, and the favored artists were showered with silver at every performance.

The people of the Comstock were generous to Civil War charities, too. One of the most unusual stories of the War is that of Reuel Gridley's sack of flour.

Gridley, who lived in Austin, sympathized with the Confederates. When he lost an election bet, he had to carry through the streets of Austin a heavy flour sack from his bakery decorated with the Union colors. By the time he had paid his bet, Gridley had become a Union man. He auctioned off the flour in Austin for $6,000 for the benefit of the Sanitary Fund (something like the present day Red Cross). Those who bought the flour gave it back to him, and Gridley traveled all over the region auctioning off his now famous sack of flour for the Sanitary Fund.

When Gridley brought his flour to Virginia City, Gold Hill, Silver City and other nearby towns, the Comstock miners bid more than $40,000 at auction for it.

Gridley's bag of flour circulated throughout Nevada. Someone called it the greatest "self-rising flour" in the country. Altogether the people of the Union states paid $275,000.00 for one sack of flour for the sake of charity. This was the first large-scale drive in the country to raise money for a particular charitable cause. The Gridley store from which the famous flour came may still be seen in Austin. The sack of flour itself is in the Nevada Historical Society Museum.

A Star on the Mountain Top

Almost from the beginning of his term in office, President Abraham Lincoln had shown particular interest in Nevada. He had sent one of his most important and influential friends, James Nye, to be Territorial Governor.

As the war went on, President Lincoln took the very unusual step

31

of proposing statehood for Nevada, which only four years before had been almost unsettled wilderness.

Lincoln's interest in Nevada proved to be one of the supreme instances of his great foresight. The President hoped to push through the Congress approval of a Constitutional amendment to abolish slavery in the United States.

As time went on he became certain he would lack the votes of one or two Senators and a Congressman to pass this important legislation. If he could create a new state adding new legislators who would be favorable to his policies, the amendment plan might succeed.

Nevada had already rejected one plan for statehood, and statehood for Nevada was also opposed by many in Congress, but the President used every kind of persuasion and influence he had to get Congress to pass an act enabling Nevada to become a state. When this was passed, Nevada quickly voted to approve statehood.

In order to get the information to the President in time, the entire new constitution was telegraphed to Washington at a cost of $3,400. This was the longest and costliest telegram ever sent, until that time.

The President proclaimed on October 31, 1864, that Nevada was now the 36th state of the United States. Henry G. Blasdel became the first Governor.

Comstock people went wild with excitement. On the back of a camel, they took a forty-foot flag to the top of the mountain, raised it on a pole there and placed a huge silver star, the thirty-sixth, on top of the pole.

For miles in every direction, people thrilled to see this symbol of Nevada's new status.

The state which came into being during the Civil War became, naturally enough, the "Battle Born State."

Collecting Your Thoughts

Find out more about how we learn the story of ancient people and about what has been discovered concerning them in Nevada.

Why did exploration in Nevada come at so much later a time than in most of the other parts of the country?

What was the secret of the Grosch brothers?

Explain the importance of Nevada during the Civil War.

33

Yesterday and Today

When Congress voted on the 13th Amendment, Nevada's first two Senators, James Nye and William Stewart, and the lone Congressman from Nevada voted for it, giving the amendment the necessary margin to pass on February 2, 1865. Sixteen days later, Nevada also became one of the first states to ratify the amendment.

President Lincoln was certain that the passage of the 13th Amendment had made unnecessary the enlistment of a million more soldiers and had saved countless lives by shortening the war, and at the same time it had freed three million slaves.

Over the years after the war, the course of Nevada history still followed for the most part the discovery of mineral riches. In various sections of the state, new strikes took the pattern of the Comstock, on a smaller scale.

Such a strike was the one at Eureka in 1864. From the silver and lead mines of Eureka came more than sixty million dollars worth of metals. So much lead was mined that for a time the lead producers of Eureka set the world market prices on lead. Substantial brick and stone buildings were built, many still in good condition today.

The ores of Eureka lasted for 90 years — longer than those of almost any other of the boom towns.

Hamilton, in Eastern Nevada, had a great strike in 1869, and was for a time the center of a population of 30,000 people. It supported 101 saloons.

After the Civil War, the great Comstock industries went on but with tremendous changes of fortune. As the little prospectors were squeezed out, power over the mines came more and more into the control of a few. Finally the big four — Mackay, Fair, Flood and O'Brien gained almost complete control and were known as the "Bonanza Kings."

Stockholders and others lost one hundred million dollars in the Comstock during the "bust of 1875." Virginia City also had a disastrous fire during that year. Another bad fire occurred in 1879.

By 1880 it became apparent that the wealth of the Comstock was rapidly diminishing. The population dwindled as people sought some other place to earn a living. No longer were the great stars of stage and music interested in coming to Virginia City. Two short decades had seen it rise to the second most important city of the West and then decline to an unimportant village.

During the period of 1880 to 1900 the population of Nevada as a whole continued to decline.

In this period the attention of the world focused on Nevada once more, even though only briefly. In 1897 Carson City was selected as the site for the world heavyweight championship boxing bout between James J. Corbett, the champion, and challenger Bob Fitzsimmons. Fitzsimmons knocked out Corbett at Carson City to become the champion. For the first time, movies were taken of the championship fight and shown around the country. They brought a million dollars to their producers — a new kind of Bonanza for Nevada.

Once Again

But if the world had thought that the days of great mining bonanzas were over in Nevada, it was mistaken.

Jim Butler, a Nevada rancher became the discoverer of Nevada's first large strike of the 20th century. The stories vary, but in the year 1900 Butler picked up some rocks, some say to throw at his burro. Instead of throwing them he thought they might have some value and kept them to be assayed. The rocks showed rich silver but not much was done for some little time. Gradually the word spread, and the Tonopah boom began.

This time the story was different, however; instead of crime and lawlessness and disorder, Tonopah regulated itself and maintained remarkable order for a frontier boom town. By 1906 the Tonopah boom was at its peak.

George Wingfield and Senator George S. Nixon combined their interests at Tonopah to form the Goldfield Consolidated Mines Company, which produced eighty million dollars in minerals. Wingfield opened many banks and built his interests until his personal fortune was estimated at fifty million dollars. He lost it all when his luck turned but again recouped with the Getchell mines income during World War II.

Altogether, the Tonopah region has yielded over 135 million dollars in mineral wealth. This could not compare with the Comstock riches, but Tonopah is still important, and many feel that its greatest mineral days are still ahead.

Nearby Goldfield became almost as wealthy and important as Tonopah. A 200 room modern hotel was built. At Goldfield in 1906, Tex Ricard staged the famous lightweight championship, bloody, 42-round fight between Joe Gans and Battling Nelson.

When the boom declined Goldfield became only a shadow of its former glory, with almost 30 blocks lined with impressive, empty buildings.

They Took A Chance

Until fairly recent years, Nevada and its people have lived somewhat away from the main course of the outside world. But a number of circumstances and events have thrown the state strongly into world attention over the past thirty or more years.

After the First World War, in which Nevadans played a loyal and important part, the country began to feel the great depression. In 1931 Nevada took a step for which it has been both praised and blamed ever since.

Gambling was made legal in Nevada. The state maintains strict control of gambling. Revenue from gambling levies provides a large part of the state's revenue needs. Because of the gambling revenues, Nevada's taxes are claimed to be the lowest in the nation. This attracts many new residents and businesses to the state.

The year 1931 saw another important beginning. Boulder City was founded to house the workers who were constructing mighty Hoover Dam. The dam itself was finished in 1936.

Once again, in 1941, the men and women of Nevada marched off to battle, as the Second World War rocked the earth. Out of that war came the atomic bomb which has a special meaning for modern Nevada.

In order to test atomic bombs, in 1951 the U. S. Government set aside a huge area of some of the most desolate acreage in Nevada as the Nevada Proving Ground of the Atomic Energy Commission. This was the nation's largest atomic testing ground. As someone has said,

Nevada passed from "silver booms to atom booms."

During the 1950's the people of Las Vegas, Tonopah, Goldfield and other surrounding towns were awed by blinding flashes of light many times brighter than daylight, shock waves making the earth tremble, and hurricanes of wind, as America's mighty modern weapons were tried out.

Overhead the now familiar mushroom clouds billowed, with red and purple flames, high into the Nevada skies, where once the only clouds would have been raised by shuffling feet of mining caravans.

Since the 1963 agreement to ban testing of atomic weapons above ground, the skies of Nevada again are blue, and the citizens of the state as well as the rest of the world hope they may remain that way. Some underground testing is still being done at the test site.

Collecting Your Thoughts

Name several ways in which the admission of Nevada as a state was different from that of most states.

Find from other sources some of the details of Nevada's celebrations at the end of the Civil War and write a short paper on this.

Tell the story of at least one other mining strike not described in this book.

Why are low taxes an advantage to Nevada?

Natural Treasures

Not all the great natural resources of Nevada are found in the earth. In spite of the fact that many people feel Nevada must necessarily be almost desolate of wild life, some of the finest and most prized fish, birds and animals are to be found in the state.

One of the most unusual fishes anywhere is found in Nevada's Pyramid Lake and nowhere else in the world. This is the Cui-Cui, upon which the Paiute Indians have depended for centuries.

The great Lahontan cutthroat trout is the only trout native to western Nevada. The world's largest catch of this fish was a 41 pound monster taken from Pyramid Lake in 1925.

Also in the productive waters of unique Pyramid Lake are found the huge landlocked salmon, so far away from the ocean and so much prized by expert fishermen.

Fishing at Pyramid Lake is controlled by the Paiutes, who have occupied the region for so long, as part of their reservation.

In the crystal clear waters of Lake Tahoe, good fishermen can outsmart Mackinaw, brown and brook trout and Kokanee salmon. Lake Mead waters provide large-mouth bass, bluegill and black crappie.

Someone has said that fishing in Walker lake is like fishing in the middle of the desert. This lake also provides fine fishing for the rare cutthroat trout, Sacramento perch, and brook trout.

Many fine mountain streams in Nevada also offer ideal fishing.

Through the Nevada skies wing some of the greatest flocks of waterfowl, for Nevada is on the great route of waterfowl migration called the Pacific flyway. Plump Canada geese, white geese, and many duck species are especially prized.

In the uplands, hunters may bag pheasant, chukar partridge, sagehen, sage grouse, and dusky grouse in season.

Seemingly completely out of place in landlocked Nevada is the pelican. Nevertheless, the largest pelican rookery in all the West is found on Anaho Island in that lake of surprises — Pyramid.

Near Fallon is found one of the largest public hunting grounds in all the Western region.

Beautiful mule deer are the most common of larger game in Nevada. Almost 10,000 deer are brought in by hunters in Nevada each year.

Deer hunting with bow and arrow is becoming more and more popular throughout the state. Elk, antelope and bighorn sheep also make Nevada their home, but they have been so reduced in numbers that even to see one of them is becoming an increasingly rare thrill. The excitement of spotting or possibly even photographing a bighorn is a rare and prized experience in the West.

Nevada has thousands of acres set aside as wildlife management areas, and many sites preserved and improved for camping.

Still A Jewel Box

Mineral wealth is still found in all parts of Nevada, just what or exactly how much not even the experts know for certain.

Many Americans are unaware of the variety, number and quality of gem stones to be found within the state. The turquoise fields of Nevada yield 87% of all the world's supplies of this precious gem. The Battle Mountain area is the world's turquoise center. Largest turquoise nugget ever found was discovered near Battle Mountain in 1954. It scaled the unbelievable weight of 152 pounds. The Crescent area near Searchlight is another important turquoise producing region.

Another of the gems found in Nevada and prized since ancient times is the opal. The largest black opal in the history of this stone was found in 1919 in the Virgin Valley opal field, near Denio. Nevada is one of the few places anywhere to produce the rare fire opal, found in Mineral, Nye, Pershing and Washoe counties as well as Virgin Valley.

Quartz, beryl, rhodonite, brucite, wonder stone, agates, geodes, jasper, petrified wood and garnet are all to be found in Nevada. The state is one of the most satisfying regions of the world for both professional and amateur gem hunters, commonly called "Rock Hounds."

Almost everyone agrees that many rich sources of gold, silver, and other valuable metals are still to be found in Nevada. In addition, and possibly even more important, substantial quantities of high grade iron ore are found in Eureka County and near Lovelock. Low grade coals are found, such as the deposits at Coaldale.

Another location for iron ore is the Lovelock region, where diatomaceous earth is also found.

The copper ores of Nevada now, perhaps, are even more prized than any other mineral.

Nevada's oil resources are not very well estimated as yet, although oil may be located in the state in future years. The oil fields of Railroad Valley in Nye County, southwest of Ely are being developed on a promising basis.

Other Resources

Nevada's broad reaches of forest are a constant surprise to visitors who expect the state to be almost treeless, which of course it is in many sections.

Large areas of the state's forest wealth are protected by the Federal Government as national forests, or are being preserved by state agencies.

The many hot springs and geysers of Nevada are another valuable asset both for their health uses and for their possible use in commercial power development.

Water is one of the most prized resources of Nevada, so scarce in some areas and so relatively plentiful in others.

In addition to the natural and artificial lakes, most of which are used at least to some extent in irrigation, there are vast reserves of ground water. Some areas can tap this ground water for irrigation and other uses simply by drilling and harnessing natural artesian flows. Others provide elaborate pumping and water distribution systems.

Collecting Your Thoughts

In addition to hunting, name other values of birds and wild animals in an area.

Find out how Nevada's minerals are located today by modern methods. Contrast this with old time prospecting.

From Hard Rocks to Cold Cash

Long before the white man came to the region we now call Nevada, centuries before any written records were kept of these happenings, the prehistoric people were finding and enjoying some of the mineral wealth already bountifully stored up in their area.

The huge mines of clear salt worked by prehistoric people of Nevada were discovered in 1926 in southern Nevada by Dr. M. R. Harrington. The Eagle Salt Works produced 334,000 tons of salt in the period of 1879 to 1884, but salt is not being produced commercially in Nevada at the present time.

Ancient peoples of Nevada also mined the wonderful turquoise and possibly even worked the potosi mine for lead. This is the earliest known mine in the state. Some believe that the early Spaniards carried on mining here, although the records are lacking. In 1855 the Mormons produced a small amount of lead there.

Washoe's Canyon produced several million dollars worth of various minerals including copper and gold before the great Comstock discoveries were known.

The Comstock was the first large-scale discovery of the state's minerals.

The Comstock has been called the richest mining strike in the history of the world. Although this is not actually the case, it certainly must rank among the richest.

Almost as important as the wealth it produced is the Comstock's contribution to the advancement of mining techniques and know-how.

For the first time in the history of metallurgy large scale hard rock mining was carried on at Virginia City. Although the rocks were rich in gold and silver, they had seemed to be locked in beyond any hope of removing them on a commercially profitable basis.

Various schemes were tried by the Comstock people. One method was to crush the ore under the hooves of mules or horses. A mine owner used this process with a team of white horses. The chemicals colored the bodies, manes and tails of the horses with multi-colored polka dots, to the amusement of the hard-bitten residents of Washoe.

Almarin Paul was certain that he could construct huge iron dish-

shaped equipment which would do the work using mechanical hammers, but most of the going mines thought the risk was too great to invest in an unknown process. Finally, Paul got the financial backing of George Hearst. Sandy Bowers and other mine operators agreed to give him a trial if he could get his mill working within the short time of sixty days to create a stamping mill.

His special equipment had to be made in San Francisco and brought over the mountains. The first steam engine in the Washoe region was trundled in, and the mill's 24 steam hammers began to pound the Comstock's ores to powder against Almarin Paul's iron dishes. It had taken just sixty days!

After being crushed, the ore was put through various processes and finally silver was separated with the use of quick silver. The bars of gleaming silver were pressed solid and ready for the outside world. At last, the Comstock was able to process its own ores without outside help.

Metal men came from many countries to study this "Washoe Process" for the refining of silver. Soon Paul enlarged and improved his plant, and other mills sprang up all over Gold Canyon. The thunder of hammers drowned out all other sounds, and the smoke of their chimneys blackened the sky.

Another real contribution of the Comstock people to mining was made by a German named Philip Deidesheimer. The very size of the ore veins in the Comstock was one of the greatest problems. The veins were so wide and deep and crumbling that no one could find a way to support the walls and ceilings while the miners worked. Many tragedies occurred when cave-ins crushed the struggling workers.

The story is told that one day Deidesheimer was watching bees at work in their hive when he suddenly thought that the way to support the mine interiors was to create a series of cells within a mine, similar to the cells of a beehive. The cells of a hive are considered to be a perfect structure.

Whether or not the story is true, Deidesheimer did work out a method of placing timbers in a manner called "square sets." These square cells could be extended into a vein up, down or sideways as far as necessary with almost perfect safety.

Deidesheimer's cells enabled the mine owners to take advantage of the Comstocks' first great bonanzas.

The square set method of timbering was used for many years in mines throughout the world.

A third great engineering accomplishment of the pioneers in the Comstock was that of Adolph Sutro. As mining progressed deeper and deeper into the earth of the Comstock, the operations became increasingly bothered by underground water, sometimes almost steaming hot from thermal areas. Often some of the most promising veins were the ones that were drowned in these underground floods.

Pumps were sometimes successful in draining the water, but Sutro was certain that the only really effective way of doing this was to build a tunnel right into the side of the mountain to reach the mining area. Once this was done the water could be run off as if from a giant spigot. This tremendous job took thirteen years to finish. By that time the Comstock prosperity had already passed its peak.

However, Sutro must be credited with one of the truly fine achievements of his day, in engineering. One of the great attractions for visitors in the region even today is to peer into the depths of what the miners sarcastically called "Sutro's coyote hole."

The mineral industry in Nevada hit its peak in 1877 and continued strong until 1879, when the Comstock declined. From 1880 until the early 1900's Nevada mining was at a low mark. Output from Tonopah and Goldfield brought a new period of mining prosperity until about 1930.

Altogether it is estimated that wealth of almost three billion dollars has come from the mines of Nevada since the early days. At present, Nevada mines bring an annual income of seventy to eighty million dollars to the state.

In 1962 the Nevada Inspector of Mines reported that there were 75 operating mines of the state employing one or more persons, with a total of 4,320 employees.

Nevada is second in production of mercury and fourth in copper among all the states.

The open cut copper mining pit at Ruth is said to be the largest in the world, and the Liberty copper pit at Ely one of the largest. Nevada's largest industry is the Kennecott Copper Corporation at McGill. Anaconda Company has a sizeable copper operation at Weed Heights.

Another large Nevada mining company is the Titanium Metals Corporation at Henderson. Mercury is the product of the Cordero Company at McDermitt.

In the 1860's the Indians showed white men a sulphur mine west of Winnemucca. This sulphur area is still being worked.

Gypsum, sand, limestone, diatomaceous earth, talc, barite, lead, zinc, perlite, pyrite, molybdenum, aragonite, magnesite, fluorspar, antimony and clay are all products of today's mining and quarrying operations in Nevada.

Green in the Desert

Ancient Indians of Nevada were the first agriculturists in the area. No one knows exactly how long ago crops were cultivated in the region, but there is plenty of evidence to show that some of the very old tribes were skilled in both irrigation and raising crops.

Others of the Indians, both ancient and more modern, depended on the nuts of the piñon trees for most of their living. Piñon nuts were ground into a nourishing flour for bread. Even today the nuts of the piñon tree are roasted and sold as a delicacy.

The Mormons were the first white farmers in Nevada. They brought with them the techniques of irrigation which had been successful in the dry lands around Salt Lake City.

Henry Dangberg irrigated his valley fields and grew hay. This feed brought as much as $300.00 a ton when supplies were scarce at the beginning of the Comstock rush.

A ship captain brought Dangberg some hay seeds from far off Chile. The farmer planted the seeds, and before long his field was covered with a deep blue-green carpet as lush looking as the fields of a tropical land. This is said to have been the first alfalfa crop grown in the United States. Today Nevada is noted for growing the finest alfalfa found anywhere.

The Dangberg Land and Livestock Company, managed by Henry Dangberg's sons, founded the town of Minden as the base of their operations.

The necessity for irrigation has been one of the limitations of Nevada agriculture, but the climate and much of the soil are excellent for growing crops, and the waters are frequently available if they can be brought to the fields.

First really large-scale reclamation program ever carried on in the United States was the Newlands Project based on the construction of Lohantan Dam in 1915.

Today, the area served by the pioneer Lohantan Reservoir, with Fallon as the marketing center, is Nevada's most important truck farm region. Heart of Gold cantaloups from Fallon rank among the world's most prized melons.

The deep layer of rich black loam left in an ancient lake bed in Lovelock Valley was only waiting for moisture to transform it into a garden. This region has been compared to that of the Nile Valley in Egypt. The Rye Patch Dam brought the needed waters, and green growing things began to encroach even into the dread forty mile desert.

At Eureka, the underground waters which flooded the mines and turned the miners to despair have become of more value than the minerals they flooded. Abundant floods from these huge underground reservoirs are now extracted to irrigate more than 40,000 acres of rich land around Eureka.

Other prominent agricultural areas in Nevada are the Moapa Valley, noted for its luscious tomatoes, so valuable they can pay their way by expensive air shipment to the markets of the East, and Pahrump Valley, known for its fine cotton.

Potatoes, onions, radishes, and the production of seed are other important agricultural activities in Nevada.

All these and other crops are now grown on a total of 727,000 acres of irrigated land in Nevada.

But far more important to Nevada agriculture than field crops is the livestock industry. Livestock accounts for 70% of Nevada farm income, and field crops only 12%, dairy products 8% and poultry 4%.

The herds of Nevada flourish whether grazing on the natural range or being fed cultivated crops such as the state's rich alfalfa hay.

Although Nevada cannot be ranked as a leading agricultural state, the average gross income of its farmers is the third highest in the United States. This is true even though the smallest proportion of its total land is cultivated as compared with other states.

The future of Nevada agriculture looks bright, however, for the climate and unused water resources appear to give crops and livestock an almost completely unused potential for growth.

Chimneys in the Desert

As in agriculture, industry in Nevada is only at the beginning of its growth.

Principal industrial city of Nevada is Henderson, a desert community. It came into being during World War II as the magnesium plant there was put into wartime operation. Pacific Engineering Company, Titanium Metals, Stauffer Chemical Company, American Potash and Chemical Corporation are among Henderson's leading firms.

Other new plants are coming to industrially undeveloped parts of Nevada, such as the Nevada Cement Company Plant at Fernley.

Some of the country's largest businesses are establishing operations in Nevada, including such organizations as North American Aviation, Aerojet-General, and Bigelow-Sanford Carpet Company.

In order to attract such business, Nevada has tried to make its tax structure the most attractive anywhere for business.

Nevada's Free Port Law is one of the principal attractions for new business. This law permits assembly and storage of products without payment of an inventory tax, under certain conditions. Nevada is the only state in the country to have such a law, and many firms are setting up warehouse and similar facilities in Nevada.

Transportation and Communication

One of the most unusual stories in all the history of publishing is that of the *Territorial Enterprise,* a newspaper which has grown up with Nevada. The *Enterprise* was founded at Genoa in 1858, only eight years after this first permanent settlement in Nevada, itself, came into being.

Later, in 1862, the newspaper was moved to picturesque Virginia City, where so much of the West's news was made.

Joseph Goodman, its owner, and the writers who worked for him all seemed to have special ability and drive which made the *Enterprise* outstanding. America's greatest humorist, Mark Twain, got his start in writing there, and many other well-known journalists served on the staff or wrote for the paper.

Before long, the *Territorial Enterprise* of Virginia City was known throughout the country and in most of Europe. Its editorials were quoted by other newspapers the world over. When actors and actresses who came to Virginia City because of its fame and generosity were given harsh criticism in the *Enterprise* it could easily wreck their careers. Many unknown artists, on the other hand, who happened to be praised by the *Enterprise,* went on to become famous simply because of it.

Although it has become a legend of journalism, it is a living legend, for the old *Territorial Enterprise* is still being published at Virginia City. For over a century its files have been one of the best sources for research into the history and legends of the West.

In its early days, the *Enterprise* often started a story with the words, "By Pony Express." This meant that the news had been carried over prairie, mountain and desert at breakneck speed by express riders, who also have become a legend of the West.

About 500 carefully selected horses and 100 of the most persistent and courageous men of the region rode the Pony Express across the dangerous wildernesses of Nevada, almost 2,000 miles from the eastern terminal at St. Joseph, Missouri. Along the way, fresh horses were ready, and the riders paused only long enough to change their mounts before clattering on again.

Danger from accident, storm or Indians was always with them. At Dry Creek, a rider once clung to life and to his horse over many miles to bring the mail in safely after being shot by Indians. He died as he reached the settlement. Another was killed as he rode, but had grasped his horse's mane so firmly they had to cut some of the mane away to loosen his hold. Together, the horse and the dead man had brought in the mail.

The Pony Express has become such a part of western history that most people find it hard to believe it only lasted a little longer than a year — from April, 1860, to October, 1861.

By this time fairly dependable telegraph service could be counted on in Nevada and the need for fast mail was not so great.

Regular stage-coach lines began to operate, and finally railroads came. In 1869 the Central Pacific Railroad was completed, and to the east, in Utah, a golden spike was driven to celebrate the first railroad to cross the United States. Now travelers and freight could cross the Nevada deserts in comparative comfort, giving little thought to the weary overland pioneers who struggled through the alkaline dust.

An English traveling lady, Isabella L. Bird, told of her trip over the transcontinental railroad shortly after it opened, starting from Truckee, California, not far from Lake Tahoe. "Precisely at 11 P.M. the huge Pacific train, with its heavy bell tolling, thundered up to the door of the Truckee House, and on presenting my ticket at the double door of a 'Silver Palace' car, the slippered steward, whispering low, conducted me to my berth — a luxurious bed three and a half feet wide, with a hair mattress on springs, fine linen sheets, and costly California blankets.

"The twenty-four passengers of the car were all invisible, asleep behind rich curtains. It was a true 'Temple of Morpheus.' Profound sleep was the object to which everything was dedicated. Four silver lamps hanging from the roof, and burning low, gave a dreamy light. On each side of the centre passage, rich rep curtains, green and crimson, striped with gold, hung from silver bars running near the roof, and trailed on the soft Axminster carpet. The temperature was carefully kept at 70°. It was 29° outside. Silence and freedom from jolting were secured by double doors and windows, costly and ingenious arrangements of springs and cushions, and a speed limited to eighteen miles an hour."

As the train crossed Nevada, Mrs. Bird continued her description, "All through that day we traveled under a cloudless sky over solitary, glaring plains, and stopped twice at solitary, glaring frame houses, where coarse, greasy meals, infested by lazy flies, were provided at a dollar per head.

"By evening we were running across the continent on a bee line, and I sat for an hour on the rear platform of the rear car to enjoy the wonderful beauty of the sunset and the atmosphere. Far as one could see in the crystalline air there was nothing but desert. The jagged Humboldt ranges flaming in the sunset, with snow in their clefts, though forty-five miles off, looked within an easy canter. The bright metal track, purpling like all else in the cool distance, was all that linked one with eastern or western civilization."

Mining regions and towns were connected to the overland railroad by short haul railroads. The most famous of these was Virginia City's own Virginia and Truckee Railroad, often called the "richest short haul railroad in United States history."

Today, some of the finest air facilities, railroads and a network of fine highways link Nevada with all the world and tie together the distant corners of the state.

Turning Water into Electricity

In addition to irrigating crops and providing water supplies for communities as far away as Los Angeles and San Diego, the waters of the Colorado River provide an enormous amount of power for the whole southwest. All this has come about through the construction of Hoover Dam and the lower dams (Parker and Imperial) downstream from it.

Building of Hoover Dam was one of the great construction achievements of its time. With a height of 726.4 feet, for many years it ranked as the highest dam in the world and still is the highest in the Western Hemisphere.

Hoover Dam was completed in the surprisingly short space of four years, under construction from 1931 to 1935. Commercial power production began in 1936. Hoover Dam's power capacity of 1,344,000 kilowatts was reached in 1961. Both Davis and Parker Dams also produce electricity.

During World War II the Hoover powerplant supplied more than half of the energy for the war production plants in southern Nevada,

HOOVER DAM drawn with Arizona wall cut away

as well as Southern California and Arizona.

The total cost of building the dam, powerplant and other facilities was 174 million dollars. Hoover Dam is self-supporting and over the years has been paying off its cost through the sale of electricity and water-storage charges. It is expected that the total cost will be paid off with income from the project.

Another Nevada source of electrical energy is a unique one, just coming into its own, although of much less capacity than Hoover Dam. This is the Beowawe Geyser field. There is great power in the hot steam of geysers. This power is now being developed by generators based on the principles used so successfully in the New Zealand geyser power operations.

Collecting Your Thoughts

Which of Nevada's resources do you expect to see develop most rapidly during the coming years? Why?

Find the reasons for the fact that mining in Nevada is not increasing.

What is the most important requirement for agriculture in Nevada?

If you had your choice to own and develop one of the many natural resources in Nevada, which one would it be? Why?

They Paved Their Streets with Silver

The men and women who made the Comstock and who in a sense were themselves re-made by the Comstock were in many ways unique in American history.

It has been said that the wealth which they created through their fantastic efforts, and often through suffering, "Built San Francisco, caused three cities to blossom and helped to win the Civil War" as well as to create a whole new approach to mining techniques.

Dozens of Comstockers became millionaires; some had possessed wealth before; others had owned absolutely nothing previously and some were illiterate.

Strangely, however, many of them, perhaps most, suffered loss of fortune, dishonor, death or some other tragedy. The theme of disaster and tragedy runs strong through all the stories of the Comstock people.

They ranged in character from the Grosch brothers, who were good, upright, gentle, kind and considerate, to such types as Sam Brown, who murdered sixteen men in the Washoe country during the winter of 1859 and 1860. The Grosches were so careful about their obligations that this trait probably cost Allen Grosch his life. He had borrowed money to pay funeral expenses for his brother Hosea. Having no money of his own, he worked to pay off this indebtedness. By the time the debts were paid, the winter had come on, making it too late to start across the mountains. When he did so in spite of the season, Allen Grosch lost his life in the perilous winter journey through cold and snow, one of the first tragedies of the Comstock, along with his brother.

In the early days on the Comstock, few women were to be found. Of those who did come in, two became particularly well known. These were Julia Bullette and Eilley Orrum.

Julia Bullette was the "Darling of the Comstock." Admirers showered her with rich gifts and attention. The Virginia City volunteer fire brigade made her an honorary member, with a dramatic-looking uniform. She went to all the fires. At the theater she sat in an exclusive box, wearing her gorgeous jewels.

But tragedy came to Julia Bullette in spite of her wealth and popularity. On a cold winter night, she was strangled by a thief, John

Millain, who wanted her jewels and furs. Julia Bullette was borne to her frozen grave while the fire brigade band played "The Girl I Left Behind Me."

They hanged John Millain for the crime, and he too went to his grave, but the women of the Comstock brought him flowers at the gallows, for they hated Julia Bullette because of the attention she received and the life she lived.

Eilley Orrum had known much poverty and hardship in her early life. During the first months, life on the Comstock was not easy. She married Sandy Bowers, her third husband, and fortune began to smile on them both. They combined their adjoining claims, which became so rich that they seemed to have all the wealth they would ever need. Their yearly income was said to be between one and three million dollars.

They set out to get the finest of everything for themselves, vowing to build the greatest mansion in the West as their new home.

Marble from far away Italy was pulled over the Sierras to build the Bowers' new mansion. Silver workers in San Francisco used silver from the Bowers' mine for every conceivable kind of household ornament, including silver hinges, door knobs, and bathroom fittings. Later they were found to be only thin silver plating. Expensive imported glass was used for windows and skylights. Water was piped from hot springs to jet up from their beautiful fountain of Spanish tile. Lace curtains at $1,200 each draped the windows. Exotic plants grew in their conservatory. The mansion is supposed to have cost more than $500,000.00.

The library was filled with good books all bound in the finest tooled Morocco leather. But the owner of the mansion had not learned to read, and many stories were told of how Sandy was never sure whether the handsome books in his library were rightside up on the shelves.

The Bowers decided to go abroad; from their ores they had made a beautiful sterling tea set to be presented to Queen Victoria, of England, with their compliments. Some say that Eilley Bowers realized her lifetime dream of being presented to the Queen, but no accurate record of this has been uncovered, and the story is believed to be only a tale.

After spending vast amounts in an attempt to gain social prestige and popularity and in purchasing many of the art treasures of the continent, they returned to Nevada and their elaborate mansion.

Soon it became plain that their claims were worked out. Sandy died in 1868 at 35 years of age, some said of a broken heart while others claimed his death was due to overwork trying to regain his fortune and prestige. He was buried on the grounds of the mansion on the hill.

Eilley lived on. She lost all the remainder of their wealth and property due to mismanagement and dishonesty of some of those around her. She had always been a mystic and believed she could foretell the future, and she even tried to earn a living by giving readings with a crystal ball. She died in poverty in 1903, alone and forgotten, and was buried beside Sandy and their adopted daughter. Today, their mansion retains much of its original appearance as headquarters for a museum.

Another of the Comstock's unhappy stories is that of the man who gave the region its name — Henry Thomas Paige Comstock. He was a disagreeable character whose ethics were often questioned, yet it seemed on many occasions that fate dealt with him more harshly than he deserved. Comstock sold his fabulous rights for $11,000 when he might possibly have had more millions than any of the others.

The first of the new millionaires to be created by the Comstock was George Hearst. Hearst had other valuable mining properties which had already been proven. He risked all of his property in the Comstock and was successful. George Hearst entered many other fields, including the newspaper business.

His son, William Randolph Hearst, was the one who expanded the family newspaper interests and built a publishing empire along with the family fame, but by this time the family had almost completely disassociated themselves from Nevada and the original source of their wealth as founded at the Comstock.

Of the big four — James Fair, James Flood, William O' Brien and John Mackay — not one kept his fortune within the state which had given him wealth and fame beyond his wildest dreams.

Mackay had come to America from his native Ireland. He found his way to the gold fields of California, but no fortune came to him there. He hurried to the Washoe country when news of the strike there reached him, but he had to take a miner's job at $4.00 a day.

When the Kentuck mine wanted to incorporate, one of their large shareholders was missing. The shareholder had been a southern sympathizer, and it was thought he might be fighting with the southern forces. John Mackay also disappeared. He never revealed where he had gone or what had happened, although some said he had actually infiltrated the southern lines to find his man, but he came back to the Comstock with the deed which had belonged to Kentuck's missing owner.

With the money he realized from the Kentuck mine, he was able to join James Fair in taking control of the Hale and Norcross mine. Their fortunes both rose and dipped in this enterprise; then they struck a bonanza vein in the 1870's, and on this vein their great fortunes were built. Mackay went on to become a communications king, building the Atlantic cable and Postal Telegraph.

These were men who loved power and authority. They sought more wealth and prestige by combining with other leaders in the field, and so Mackay and Fair joined with William O'Brien and James Flood. Together they operated 3,000 feet of the Comstock adjoining the Hale and Norcross.

Their explorations soon reached the greatest bonanza of them all, a property which they called the Consolidated Virginia and California Mines. In the short five years between 1874 and 1879, Consolidated Virginia and California brought the incredible sum of $100,000,000.00 in dividends to its shareholders. In this way the creation of the "Big Four" of Comstock's Bonanza Kings came about. The wealth and influence they gained on Nevada's slopes eventually reached the far corners of the world.

James Fair went on to become United States Senator from Nevada for the term beginning in 1881. However, he used his wealth primarily as one of the great builders of San Francisco.

John Mackay died in 1901. Mrs. Mackay and their son Clarence founded the Mackay School of Mines at Reno. This fine institution has as its aim the improvement of the industry which brought the Mackays their fortune. In later years the Mackay family gained great social prominence and influence both in the United States and in Europe.

Men of Enterprise

Virginia City was not yet three years old when the *Territorial Enterprise* was installed in a fine new brick headquarters building. Its influence had become immense. *Enterprise* owner, Joe Goodman, kept fully in touch with both local and outside news. He had great ability and he surrounded himself with newspaper men of ability. The things they wrote were read with appreciation and respect.

In 1862 Goodman published an article by a miner at Aurora, who signed his name "Josh." Josh wrote in a witty and sarcastic way about a local judge who was so full of self-importance it was "impossible to

print his lectures in full, as the type-cases had run out of capital I's."

Other articles by Josh were sent to the *Enterprise,* and finally in August, 1862, Goodman offered Josh a job on his paper. Josh, it turned out, was a young man named Samuel Clemens. He had come west with his older brother, Orion Clemens, who had been appointed Secretary of the Nevada Territory.

Previously Samuel had tried his hand at many jobs. He had been a pilot on the Mississippi River, had worked with his brother in his print shop in Iowa and had tried his hand at prospecting in Nevada. But he had never been a writer.

This job gave Clemens his start in writing. It was the custom in those days for writers to assume a name, and so on February 2, 1863, one of the great names in American literature was "born." For the first time Samuel Clemens signed an article "Mark Twain."

Mark Twain realized that frontier men wanted humor more than anything else to help them break away from the realities of their drab and often dangerous life. So he started to dream up the witty and often ridiculous stories for which he later became so famous. Even as a writer on the Enterprise, some of his stories gained world attention.

At Virginia City, Twain met all the famous people who were flocking to the Comstock, such as the great humorist Artemus Ward. Twain became acquainted with the great and humble alike and stored up a knowledge of the characters of the Washoe area to last him a lifetime.

When Goodman sent Mark Twain to the territorial legislature as a reporter, he soon made such an impression and had gained so many friends that he boasted he had more influence on the legislature as a simple reporter than any of the members of legislature themselves. His humor could get things done when arguments and logic failed.

In May of 1864 Mark Twain offended the editor of a rival newspaper, and the code of the West called for a duel. Neither man was anxious to meet the other on the dueling field. Twain knew nothing about dueling pistols, but there seemed to be no way out of it. Mark Twain challenged the editor, and he accepted, but when the time came the editor refused to fight.

Just when it looked as if Mark Twain was the hero, word came that he was to be arrested for violating the legislature's new law against dueling, and he left Nevada forever, a fugitive from justice of the area he liked so well.

Samuel Clemens had been on the staff of the *Enterprise* less than two years, but it had given him the start toward becoming one of the great writers of all time. He had not been too kind to Nevada or to its people in his writings, but they are still proud of giving Mark Twain to the world.

The *Enterprise* produced several other well-known literary talents. William Wright, who used the name Dan De Quille, created a number of famous hoaxes. One of these was about an imaginary scientific discovery De Quille was supposed to have made in the Washoe country. Scientists from all over the world begged to know more about his research. Even the great showman Barnum made him an offer to demonstrate his imaginary process.

De Quille's book "Big Bonanza," published in 1878, was the first full-scale history of the Comstock.

Rollin M. Daggett was another of the prominent *Enterprise* men.

No one of the employees, however, was more remarkable than their boss, Joe Goodman. He realized that frontier journalism was different from any other. He said all his reporters had to shoot straight with both gun and pen. He believed his newspaper should tell the truth as it saw it, even if "injured" people should try to take vengeance on Goodman or on his staff, as they often did.

It was no accident that an obscure frontier paper should become one of the famous names in journalism. It had some of the most remarkable men of journalism to build it.

The Twain Shall Meet

When President Lincoln appointed Orion Clemens to be Secretary of Nevada Territory, the new Secretary was so penniless he could not afford to make the trip from Missouri to take his job in far off Nevada. Secretary Clemens was forced to borrow money from his younger brother Sam. Of course this was before Sam had become the famous

Mark Twain, but Sam had saved some money from his work as a river pilot.

So the two brothers, using Sam's savings, set out for what was to them a completely unknown land. Orion had promised to make Sam his personal secretary, but when they reached Nevada they found there was no provision for such a position, so Sam was on his own.

Orion Clemens proved to be a good Territorial Secretary. He ran things with great economy and with considerable efficiency. He even created a handsome design for the Nevada territorial seal.

Governor Nye was away from Nevada a great part of the time. He spent many of his days in the pleasanter climate of California and left Orion in charge as acting governor.

This pleased Orion, his wife Molly and his brother Mark Twain very much. They all liked the prestige which came from such a high position. Molly Clemens became the social leader of Carson City, and the new home built by Orion was among the finest in the area at the time.

The first cloud on this happiness was the death of their only daughter, Jane, from dreaded RockyMountainspotted fever. Before she died she had been been saving her pennies to buy a Bible. The Clemens, who were very active in the First Presbyterian Church, bought a Bible in her memory and presented it to the church where it is still in use today. Jane Clemens was buried in a grave in Lone Mountain cemetery.

From that point on, Orion Clemens life seemed to diminish. When the new state government came into being, his job as Territorial Secretary was finished. He left Nevada and tried many jobs but with slight success.

Meanwhile his brother, Mark Twain, had become internationally known and helped to support Orion and his wife. Mark had a very large income from his writing. In later years Mark Twain also had difficulty with his finances, and these two brothers, both with such great ability, spent their later years in much unhappiness.

Both brothers could look back to their days in Nevada as being among the happiest and most rewarding they had spent, when they both "governed" the territory, each in his own way.

According to historian Effie Mona Mack, "The people of Nevada can be grateful to Secretary Orion Clemens for his patience, sacrifice and work in getting the Territory of Nevada organized."

A "Saint" on the Snow

Marking a grave at Genoa is a most remarkable monument, topped by two skis carved in stone. This indicates the final resting place of John A. Thompson, who has become a sort of "patron saint" of American skiers.

Thompson came to America from his native Norway in 1837 and made his way to California in 1851. He heard of the difficulties of carrying the mail through the high Sierra Nevadas. He knew of the methods of traveling over snows in his homeland. He thought he could manage to carry the mails quickly and safely.

In 1856 he made his first journey with the mail, from Placerville in California, to Genoa. This was a ninety mile struggle of extraordinary difficulty, over rough ground, up mountain slopes and through the enormously deep Sierra snows. Sometimes his mail sack weighed as much as eighty pounds.

Thompson never carried blankets, and his only food was dried meat. He would catch short naps, simply lying down in the snow, then would push on to keep his circulation up.

For the incredible period of twenty years, John Thompson carried the mails over this route, sometimes bringing much needed medicines, as well.

But the most memorable fact about John Thompson is his pioneer use of skis. He is supposed to have been the first person in the United States to use them. Snowshoes had been used by the Indians in America for centuries before the time of the white man, but skis were a European invention. Although Thompson was nicknamed "Snowshoe" Thompson, he used true skis, which he created himself, not snowshoes. His skis were ten feet long, six inches wide and weighed twenty-five pounds.

Today, skiers all over America owe a debt of gratitude to Snowshoe Thompson who demonstrated the value of skis for twenty pioneering years.

Three Senators from Nevada

James Warren Nye was prominent in New York politics, and President Lincoln is said to have felt that he received the New York vote in the 1860 Presidential election principally due to Nye's work.

Lincoln is supposed to have appointed Nye Governor of Nevada Territory out of gratitude for his help in the election. This might have seemed a rather unimportant appointment compared to a high national post, but Nye apparently felt he could build a great future in this position. In his first speech in Nevada he declaimed "I have come to this distant country with the hope of adding one more bright and glorious star — Nevada." It would seem he already had in mind the prospect of statehood for Nevada.

The Governor appointed to various offices as many of his political friends as he possibly could. His assistants had assistants, and sometimes they had assistants too. When the governor sailed from New York for Nevada, by way of Panama and San Francisco, his party practically filled the ship. They had so much baggage one ship could not hold it all. Some of it had to wait for the next ship.

When James Nye first reached the new territory of Nevada where he was to be Governor, he was given a great reception, and his first remark is said to have been: "I was told that I was coming into a wild and dangerous country but, on the contrary, I find here the most hospitable people I ever met."

Of course, the Nevadans were delighted, and this remark was typical of one of the nation's most unusual political experts. James Nye knew almost better than anyone else "how to make friends and influence people."

He quickly gained friends throughout the territory, making many appointments to government posts.

As Nevada grew and prospered, he saw his hopes for high position becoming brighter all the time, with the growing prospects of statehood. In May of 1864 he wrote to President Lincoln an interesting description of early Nevada: "Churches have been built, school houses erected and in almost every town in the territory substantial improvements in every branch of industry are made. . . . Obstacles that would seem insurmountable in many places here seem only to quicken the zeal and energies of our people.

"Mountains are tunnelled; shafts are sunk thousands of feet through solid rock; rivers are turned from their channels; canals are made, conducting water for fifty or sixty miles; roads are constructed over the highest mountain peaks with a wonderful facility and rapidity; mines are opened and quartz mills erected as if by magic; cities spring up like the 'gourd in the night.'"

When Nevada became a state, James Nye was chosen by the Legislature to be one of the first two United States Senators from Nevada. The high national office he had sought so long was his at last.

The *Chicago Tribune* described Nye as a Senator: "He is the best speaker on instantaneous occasions in the United States . . . His cunning and his good nature glide into and conceal each other."

Nye was re-elected to the Senate in 1867 but was defeated in 1873 and left Nevada forever. Not long afterward he suffered a stroke, was sent to an asylum and died in New York state in 1876. A Nevada newspaper said at his death, "To write a full and fitting obituary notice of James W. Nye would be to write the history of the Republican Party; the story of the administration of Abraham Lincoln; the struggle of the Union; the scheme of Reconstruction and the life and achievements of the Republican Party of the State of Nevada. Our dead friend and neighbor was as closely united to all these momentous matters and events as any man of his day. . . ."

Among his belongings after his death was found a note which read: "Dear General — come up tonight and swap jokes. Lincoln."

William Morris Stewart was one of the most forceful characters of the West. He brought a massive physique and strong character to Nevada when he came to the Washoe region from California. Bill Stewart had been successful in California, had even been the Attorney General of that state, but he saw greater prospects in the new lands around the Comstock.

Stewart brought his Yale training and tremendous talent for straightening out difficult situations to the complicated problems of mining claims around Virginia City.

He is said to have become a millionaire through the rich fees he earned as a lawyer, trying to protect his clients' rights in their claims. There were sometimes so many claims and counter-claims to rich mining rights that the lawyers often cleared more from their fees than the owners did for their mining rights. Many a rich claim was lost and many another fortune made in the courts.

Stewart, as well as Nye, saw Nevada statehood as his great chance for advancement. He had long ago determined that he would become one of the first Senators from Nevada.

The state constitution and the success of the second constitutional convention were largely due to his efforts. He was one of the most energetic and tireless of workers.

During that period, United States Senators were chosen by the state legislatures, not elected by the people. When the time came for the Nevada Legislature to choose Nevada's first two United States Senators, Stewart was the only man who could count on the election almost without question.

One of Nevada's first Senators would have a four year term, the other six. Stewart and Nye agreed to cast lots for the six-year term. As it almost always did, Fortune favored Bill Stewart, and he became the full-term Senator. He served for two terms. Then in 1887 he was again elected Senator and served until 1905. His remarkable span of public service to Nevada stretched from territorial days into the twentieth century. Possibly his greatest national accomplishment was the authorship of the 15th amendment to the U.S. Constitution. This amendment assures citizens of the U.S. the right to vote "regardless of race, color or previous condition of servitude." He also was the author of the National Mining Code.

One of Stewart's most interesting memories, and one of the most interesting for the people of Nevada was of the day of April 14th, 1865, in Washington. Senator Stewart had gone to the White House late that afternoon to introduce a friend to President Lincoln. When Stewart sent his card in to the President, Lincoln turned it over and wrote on the back, "I am engaged to go to the theater with Mrs. Lincoln. It is the kind of an engagement I never break. Come with your friend tomorrow at ten and I shall be glad to see you."

As President Lincoln got into his carriage, Senator Stewart was standing at the door with his friend, who was introduced and who shook the President's hand. Then Lincoln shook Senator Stewart's hand and said, "Come back in the morning." And the carriage pulled away.

That note and good-by to Senator Stewart are generally supposed to have been the last note and the last farewell message of the great man who a few hours later became the first American President to be assassinated.

Another of Nevada's best-known United States Senators was James G. Scrugham. He came to Nevada in 1917 to be Dean of the State University's Engineering College. He was elected Governor of Nevada in 1923, then served in the national House of Representatives from Nevada from 1933 until 1942. He became a Senator in 1943 and served until his death in 1945. Senator Scrugham is often credited with being the leading figure in the development of the Colorado River by means of the Hoover Dam.

A Messiah and a Chief

Nevada's Mason Valley was the boyhood home of one of the most unusual Indians in American history. This was Jack Wilson who was called the "Paiute Messiah" because he hoped to save his people and their lands from the onrushing white man.

His strange teachings were designed to convince his people that he had the power to make the white man disappear from the land, if his people would only give him their help. He created strange ceremonials designed to cause the white man to evaporate. These closed with the eerie Ghost Dance.

The unrest which Jack Wilson and his teaching caused finally resulted in an uprising of the Sioux in 1890. The famed chief Sitting Bull, who had massacred General Custer, was killed in this 1890 uprising.

The most famous Indian name in Nevada history is probably that of the Chief Old Winnemucca of the Paiutes. The Nevada city of Winnemucca was renamed in his honor. This strong, stern leader was proud of his power and authority, but throughout his life he remained a friend of the white man, and it is probable that white and Indian relations in Nevada were far better because of Winnemucca than they otherwise could ever have been.

Collecting Your Thoughts

Why do you suppose life and fortunes were so uncertain on the Comstock?

Find out more about where the wealth taken from the Comstock was spent or invested. Why do you think most of it left the state?

On what was the influence of the Territorial Enterprise built?

If you could choose a friend from among the prominent Nevadans of the past, who would it be? Why?

71

Teaching and Learning

Education in Nevada has changed greatly since Virginia City's first teacher, Harry Floty, kept six pistols and a bowie knife on his desk.

Education in the western states has always been taken seriously. Generally the West spends more money per pupil in education than most of the eastern states. Westerners insist on the highest qualifications for their teachers. Nevada follows the western pattern in all of this.

One of Nevada's proudest possessions is the beautiful University of Nevada at Reno, with a campus overlooking two scenic mountain ranges — the Virginia Mountains and the lofty Sierra Nevadas, with the placid Truckee Meadows at the front door.

The University of Nevada has the general advantages of state universities in other states, but because Nevada is a small state its pupils have the added advantage of a smaller and more intimate place in which to gain a higher education, with the assistance of the highly qualified faculty of a state university.

Begun at Elko in 1874, the University was moved to Reno in 1885, where its campus covers 76 acres on a plateau. It is one of the original land-grant schools.

A southern regional division of the University was established at Las Vegas in 1956 and now has an enrollment almost as large as the parent campus at Reno.

One of the University's most unique accomplishments is the creation of the Atmospherium-Planetarium, opened in November, 1963. Its modern building is called a "space age structure" because of its unusual design as it rises from the desert scenery on a bluff overlooking the Reno campus.

The Atmospherium is the only one of its kind in the world. A specially designed camera with a 180-degree wide-angle lens has been developed to take color motion pictures of the sky from horizon to horizon, with scientific care and accuracy. These are projected on and completely over the special dome of the building. The weather of a whole day can be speeded up and shown in only a few minutes, as the projector throws its pictures on the dome.

In addition, the stars and other features of the night skies are

projected on the dome in the more traditional manner by a planetarium projector.

Dr. Wendell A. Mordy, director of the University's Desert Research Institute was responsible for the development of this extraordinary facility. The Max C. Fleischmann Foundation provided necessary funds, and the cost was about $500,000.00.

Of course, the Desert Research Institute itself is also a remarkable institution.

Also a part of the University at Reno is the Mackay School of Mines, founded by the Mackay family in honor of Mr. Mackay. This has long been considered one of the finest of all institutions in its field.

Collecting Your Thoughts

Would you prefer to attend a very large or a small college or university? Why?

Why is it particularly appropriate that one of the country's finest schools of mining should be located in Nevada?

Enchantment of Nevada

From Silver Booms to Atom Booms

Nevada has been called a "land of contrasts." Here visitors find the most sophisticated stage shows not far from the most primitive Indian reservations. Pioneer days are remembered in more than a hundred mining camps now existing only as ghost towns. These may be found in the same state with Las Vegas, where Fremont Street is said to have more lights and neon signs than Broadway in New York. Here is a land where the burro's feet once bled from tramping on the silver ore to crush it and where today pampered white burros may be hired as caddies on a golf course, treading only on luxurious sod.

The past in Nevada is particularly interesting to the visitor because the past seems so much more real in a state where more of the old West has survived than anywhere else. In the ghost towns, whether restored or in sad decay, visitors seem to feel themselves carried back to the old days. Someone has called a ghost town a place "where the floodtide of life has receded."

Ghost towns in fact are considered to be a "Nevada trademark."

The sense of history is strong all through Nevada, where history has been strange and unusual.

Much that visitors find different about Nevada today is rooted strongly in its history. Gambling has flourished since pioneer days, and the character of Nevada's people has always been that of independence and of letting a neighbor do what he pleased without prying into his affairs.

Nevadans also point to the fact that the state has more churches per capita than any other state. Residents believe this fact helps to reveal the character of their "Sagebrush State."

In Spanish, the word Nevada means "snow-covered."

More than eighty-five per cent of the state's area is owned by the Federal Government. There are a National Recreational Area — Lake Mead — and a National Monument — Lehman Caves — in the "Silver State," and part of another National Monument — Death Valley — all within Nevada's borders.

Nine state parks are now in operation for the benefit of residents and visitors alike.

One of the state's slogans is "Recreation unlimited," and the activities and interesting features of the state do cover almost everything from scenery of greatest variety to such sports as skiing, both water and snow, in the state where snow skiing came to America.

According to Robert Warren, Director of the Nevada Department of Economic Development, 18 million people visit Nevada yearly to take advantage of these attractions.

A "Dream of Beauty"

For the visitor who wants to follow the best-worn paths of early history, the way over the Sierra Nevadas will serve as a constant reminder of the eager prospectors who struggled across the mountain heights and through snows in their search for riches.

Nestled between California and Nevada, and shared by them, is one of the world's most beautiful and best-known lakes. Tahoe is the largest high-altitude lake on the North American continent. Its crystal waters are so clear that an object can be seen clearly 65 feet straight down. Fishermen often complain about the clarity of the water, where fish can see their would-be captors so easily. Nevertheless, fishing is one of the most popular activities of the Tahoe region, along with water skiing, boating, and swimming at such beaches as beautiful Sand Harbor State Beach.

Visitors to Tahoe enjoy the novelty of Cal-Neva Lodge, which is on the state line. There gambling can be carried on only in the part of the lodge on the Nevada side.

The Mile-High Regatta is one of the most popular attractions of the Tahoe region.

Kit's Town

The Capital of Nevada is only a short distance away from Tahoe in these high-speed days, but once the journey was long and often one of real danger.

Carson City, smallest of all United States Capitals, was founded by Abe Curry in 1858 and was first known as Eagle Ranch. It was renamed in honor of the famous western scout, Kit Carson. Although

the city had been the Capital for many years, it was not incorporated until 1875.

The capitol building was begun in 1870, and the state legislature met there in 1871. The eight months time required to complete this splendid capitol are contrasted with the 18 or 20 years often needed to complete other state capitols.

Long rafters of hewn logs combined with native stone quarried at the state prison have created a sturdy Nevada Capitol. It is one of the most simple, dignified and charming of all the capitols.

Wainscoting, arches and floors in the capitol are of Alaskan marble blocks weighing 20 tons each. These were shipped from Alaska to Richmond, California, where they were sawed and polished. Then they were transported to Carson City.

An unusual decorative frieze more than 400 feet long extends along the length of the main corridor. At the top of the frieze is a border of pine cone design and at the bottom a border of grapevines, showing the contrast from north to south in the state. The main portion of the frieze represents Nevada's products, industries and symbols.

Pride of the capitol building is the wonderful portrait of Abraham Lincoln from which the Lincoln likeness on the five dollar bill was taken. This picture was painted in 1911 by Charles Sean and purchased by the state for the 50th anniversary of statehood. It is considered one of the finest portraits of the President who brought statehood to Nevada.

The grounds of the capitol cover four beautifully landscaped blocks within Carson City. The ornate iron fence enclosing the grounds was installed in 1875 at a cost of only $5,000 in only one month's time. Some-one has said that the reason it was built so well in such a short time at such a low cost was because the low bidder who got the contract for the job was a woman school teacher, Hannah K. Clapp.

One of the principal attractions of Carson City is the Nevada State Museum. From 1870 to 1893 the building of the museum served as a branch of the United States Mint, where the precious metals of Washoe and other regions were turned into $50,000,000 worth of coins. When there was no further need for a mint there, the building was used as a federal assay office until 1933. In 1939 the state of Nevada pur-chased the federal building and turned it into a museum which was dedicated in 1941.

The most spectacular exhibit, appropriately, is the "mine." The old mint vaults were converted into 300 feet of mining "tunnels." Here full-scale exhibits of mining operations are housed. Hoisting, drilling, blasting and other common Nevada mining practices are shown.

Mementoes of the Battleship Nevada, including the ship's silver used in two world wars, are displayed at the museum, and Nevada's wealth of minerals is represented in the Mineral Room.

The Indian Room shows, among other materials, some of the won-derful baskets of Dat-So-La-Lee, the Washoe basketmaker.

One of the first churches in Nevada, the First Presbyterian, is an-other landmark sought out by many Carson City visitors. The first church in Nevada was finished at Virginia City in 1861 and was of the Methodist denomination.

A Vanished Luster

For most visitors, the path of history takes them the short fifteen miles from Carson City to Virginia City. In fact, the "population" of this most lively of all ghost cities is larger now than it ever was if the 50,000 visitors per week are counted. This astonishing horde travels to Virginia City trying to recapture the exciting days there. As visitors wander the historic streets, most must be thinking of the 30,000 adventurous men and women who created in three short years what Lucius Beebe called the "Cosmopolis of the West," where almost a billion dollars poured into the country's economy, where four banks, six churches, 100 saloons and gambling houses, an opera house and even an elevator had sprung up over night on a desert slope.

Today the roads are no longer paved with discarded low-grade silver ore from the mines. Traces of this might still be found, but there are many other reminders of the life that once was.

Well-maintained St. Mary of the Mountains Catholic Church is one. Its silver bell was cast in far off Spain, where metal from the Comstock was shipped for its casting. St. Mary's Italian marble altar, rosewood pillars and blue ceilings are further evidence of the longing for beauty which was felt so strongly in the rough surroundings of the mining camps.

The *Territorial Enterprise* still operates in the historic building where so many well known desks have stood. Its files are of great value to many who study the history of the West.

Yet in spite of Virginia City's active present, few can escape the feeling that here is a place rooted in the past where memories predominate of the great stage and music stars, of Mark Twain, of brave Reverend Franklin Rising, of the Bonanza Kings, of tragic Eilley Bowers, of Julia Bullette, of Hank Monk the stage driver, of Bill Stewart, and even of the roughnecks and murderers — all who played a part in Virginia City's unique history.

All this is brought home even more strongly by a visit to the lonely grave of Hosea Grosch, the ill-fated young man who with his equally ill-starred brother almost made all of it their own.

Other graves nearby may also be seen — those of Sandy and Eilley Bowers, on the cliff behind their mansion in the wilderness. Today that mansion is a county museum with fine recreational facilities, and it has been beautifully restored.

Not Only by Chance

To many people there is something completely right in the fact that even Reno's name was chosen by lot, for its gambling and divorce law have made its name known throughout the world. But its citizens are quick to point out that there are more couples married in Reno than are divorced there. The six-weeks divorce law has been on the books since 1931. A few prominent divorces under the system brought it international attention, and the throng of easy-divorce seekers have been coming ever since to the pleasant city on the Truckee Meadows.

The building of the transcontinental railroad was responsible for Reno's founding in 1868. The permanent residents of Reno and vicinity are solid citizens. Some mining families tracing their fortunes to the early mineral strikes live there quietly. The city is the center for a large community of Basque ranchers of fine reputation, who have established their "dynasties" in the region.

Other ranchers, cattlemen and mining operators help make Reno a center of business activity.

One of the main tourist attractions of Reno is its annual rodeo. During rodeo time anyone not wearing western clothes is given a token fine.

Also of particular interest to tourists is the museum of the Nevada Historical Society in the State Building. Here may still be seen the historic sack of flour sold by R. C. Gridley so many times for so many thousands of dollars.

The museum is said to have the finest collection in all the West of Indians and prehistoric peoples. Here is the finest group of exhibits from the discoveries in Lovelock Cave, with samples of almost every type of item found there. A unique picture of Dat-So-La-Lee at work is part of the museum's collection on the famed basket-maker.

Another interesting collection at the museum shows the ingenuity of the mining pioneers. They wanted musical instruments for their dances. When there were none to be had, they made their own. The museum shows a bass viol made from a child's bathtub, a cello from an old oil can and a banjo from a school clock, among others.

The campus of the State University attracts many visitors. This place of beauty was created from the desert, with artificial lakes and landscaping. The Atmospherium-Planetarium is a tourist attraction on the campus, and many visitors make it a point to see the splendid statue of John Mackay, by the famed sculptor Gutzen Borglum.

Near Reno, the Ski Bowl claims to have the world's biggest chair lift, and another Reno neighbor, Sparks, is now one of the state's largest residential communities.

Other Western Points of Interest

Cradled in the desert north and east of Reno is mysterious Pyramid Lake, given its name by Fremont because of the volcanic rock islands which jut from its surface in pyramid shape. Today the lake is part of the Pyramid Lake Indian Reservation. The Indians control the area, as they have since long before its history was recorded.

This inland sea is surrounded by colorful rock cliffs, its weird appearance, with steam floating from hot springs at many points, has given rise to many legends, and this desert lake with its exclusive cui-cui fish and other good fishing is a unique travel experience. It has no outlet.

Another desert sea without an outlet is Walker Lake, named for early explorer Joseph Walker, who found it in 1833. Hawthorne is the center for fishermen seeking Walker Lake's famed cutthroat trout. At Hawthorne you can always count on a free parking space for your burro, as provided by the city laws. The ghost towns of Aurora and Rawhide are best explored from Hawthorne. Hawthorne is also the site of the nation's largest ammunition depot.

The all-year flying weather at Fallon has made it the location of a Naval Auxiliary Air Station. To the east, the rustle of sand carried along on the wind has given Singing Sand Mountain its name. The earthquake faults east of Fallon are said to be the most spectacular in the world. Lake Lahontan, with good fishing, marks the nation's first large scale reclamation project, keeping 70,000 acres green by capturing and holding the runoff of Sierra snows for later use on the fields.

At Lovelock, immigrant parties in the early days prepared for the terrible crossing of the Forty-Mile Desert. The Lovelock region flourished because of beavers which had dammed the Humboldt River, providing water for irrigation. It was not until generations later that human engineers threw up the Rye Patch Dam to do the same job. Huge steam blowers are spectacles of Brady's Hot Springs. The most spectacular of these resulted from the drilling of two thermal steam-power wells.

The Lovelock caves were the scene of some of the most important archeological discoveries in the whole region. This important find was made accidentally by miners who were working the bat guano of the cave. Thousands of important items relating to prehistoric people have been taken from the cave, including feathered articles, baskets, wooden implements, sandals, woven bags and mummies.

Attractions to the North and East

Another Humboldt River city, Winnemucca, namesake of the Indian chief, is the trading center for much of Northern Nevada and for some of southern Idaho as well. A government early-warning radar station perches atop Winnemucca Mountain, in contrast to the old Chinese cemetery at Winnemucca, where the Indians used to gather during a burial, waiting to steal the ceremonial meat brought by the

Chinese to serve their departed countryman on his way to his ancestors.

Winnemucca is the site of the Nevada Rodeo, considered one of the best in the West.

A large Basque sheepherding population is found around Winnemucca, and Basque dishes are common in the restaurants there.

Winnemucca was the scene of one of the earliest labor strikes. Freight companies did a thriving business carrying supplies to nearby mining regions by mule team. In 1874 the drivers called a strike asking five cents per pound on freight.

To the east Beowawe geysers provide an eerie display of the forces at work underground in the largest geyser basin in the United States outside of Yellowstone Park.

Mormon crickets are found in the region around Carlin in such numbers that motorists are fearful at times that the insects' slippery bodies on the roads will cause skids as bad as those on ice. Of course, the crickets also worry the farmer. They can cause extensive crop damage.

Elko is the most important cattle town in Nevada, center of great ranches. It hails Bing Crosby as its Honorary Mayor and movie actor Jimmy Stewart as Honorary Sheriff. The city has been carefully designed with false store fronts to make it look like a pioneer cattle town of the 1880's. The name Elko means "one woman" in the Indian language. This was the cry Indian squaws used to warn other squaws when they saw white men coming with only a few women in their party.

On the Nevada-Utah line is Wendover, half of the town in one state and half in the other. Wendover residents may live on the Utah side, but they have to come to the Nevada part to do their gambling. Wendover is the supply center for the world-famous Utah Salt Flat racing area.

Other important eastern Nevada towns are Ruth and Ely. John Ely bought his mine for $3,500.00, and he earned twenty million dollars from it. Ely and Ruth form one of the most important copper communities in the United States, with the Liberty Copper Pit mine at Ruth often called the world's largest open pit type of operation. At sunset, visitors to this pit are reminded of the Grand Canyon. The cut is classed among the largest engineering works of man.

The annual Pony Express Days at Ely are very spectacular, with such events as an Indian uprising, a stage coach robbery, street dancing and horse racing.

To the east is Lehman Caves National Monument, named for the caves' discoverer, Absolom Lehman, a pioneer homesteader in the region. Skeletons and other evidence show that ancient peoples also knew of the caves. The National Monument was established in 1922. Visitors' trails half a mile long have been developed and almost two miles of passageways have been explored within these wonderful caverns.

Over thousands of years, dripping water has formed fantastic rock shapes throughout the cave. The method of formation of some of these is a complete puzzle to geologists. One of the most unusual formations is the ribbonlike "bacon strips." Graceful draperies, organ pipes, artists' palettes, terraced pools, fluted columns, crystal mushrooms and chocolate-colored pillars are among the countless formations preserved in Lehman Caves.

Central and Southern

The miners and prospectors who built Eureka were sure it was go-

ing to last, and so they put up substantial buildings which are still being used by the bustling town today. They were rewarded with the longest continuous production record of any mining area in the state. Today the 10,000 people who earned their living in the mines, the 150 saloons, the opera house with famous stars, are only memories, but Eureka is the center of other activities.

Another famed mining name of central Nevada is Austin, where one of the early buildings had a stairway which could be swung up out of the way of floods from the frequent cloudbursts.

Lander County Court House at Austin is the oldest in the state, and the local newspaper, *Reese River Reveille,* has been published since 1863. It is still edited from the original editor's desk. Austin was the home of Emma Wixon, who became a famous American soprano, using the name Emma Nevada.

Ichthyosaur Paleontological State Monument offers the only display of its kind in the nation. Here the remains of huge fish-like reptiles, which grew up to sixty-feet long, possibly 180 million years ago, can be seen just where they were first discovered and uncovered. Bones of six of the ichthyosaurs have been exposed to plain view just where eons ago they must have been washed ashore and stranded in some prehistoric sea, to become petrified and endure even to the present day. Parts of thirteen others have been excavated nearby.

Ichthyosaur Monument is in Nye County, the third largest county in the United States. One of the most unusual natural formations anywhere is Diana's Punch Bowl, also in Nye County.

Four of Nevada's most famous mining towns are found in the southern sector — Tonopah, Goldfield, Rawhide and Pioche.

Rawhide sprang up with Goldfield, had a brief fling as a rip-roaring boom town and declined until today it is almost deserted, a perfect example of its type. Goldfield has been called the last of the boom towns, but it failed to become a ghost town, and lives on as the county seat and tourist and shopping center. Tonopah, too, continues although to a considerably lessened extent. The old Tonopah Club and Mizpah Hotel remain as tourist attractions. Adding a modern touch to Tonopah is its air base.

Pioche was called the most trigger-happy town in eastern Nevada. It sprang up in the middle of nowhere, 300 miles from another town. The Pioche of today has its "million dollar courthouse" and crowded boot hill to remind all comers of the rowdy and exciting past. Seventy-five people died violent deaths at Pioche before there was the first natural death at the town.

Near Pioche is awesome Cathedral Gorge State Park, a vast chasm where the principal feature is the great towers of rock, looking like imposing church towers or lofty skyscrapers. These formations have been sculptured over the centuries by wind and water in a narrow gorge.

Another state park which shows off the natural wonders of the state is Valley of Fire. Here Nature has carved a wonderland of strange forms from the red sandstone, and as the sun sets, the walls of the valley light up with the red glow of a vast, hot fire.

Two of the most famous rock formations in Valley of Fire are the Elephant Rock and Donald Duck, a rock of vast size with a neck and snout almost too much like the original to be believed.

In the Valley of Fire, are found the pictures made on the rocks by ancient peoples who considered this mysterious area a sacred place. Still to be seen are the carvings of rocky-mountain sheep made by ancient artists. Apparently these prehistoric people would draw in advance a picture of the animal they wanted to kill, in the hope this would help in the coming hunt.

A petrified forest is another attraction of the region.

Not far away, at Overton, is Lost City Museum. Here were taken many of the relics of an ancient Indian pueblo. Today this priceless town of centuries past lies buried under the water of Lake Mead.

But while the waters of Lake Mead covered up the remains of an old civilization, they created a new one in the heart of the desert.

Boating, fishing, water skiing, swimming, scuba diving and all the other joys of a large body of water are now available in a desert setting because of this greatest of all man-made lakes.

One of Lake Mead's principal attractions is the Sahara Cup Races for large hydroplanes, held each year.

The massive concrete stopper which keeps Lake Mead corked up in its valley — Hoover Dam — is also a great tourist attraction. Fast elevators take visitors 528 feet into the heart of the huge structure. This distance is equal to the height of a 44 story building.

Nearby Boulder City is of particular interest because it was completely planned as a model city before being built. Boulder City was owned by the Federal government until it was incorporated as a part of Nevada in 1959. Unusual in Nevada, especially so close to Las Vegas, is the fact that there is no gambling here and no liquor is sold.

Not Merely by Chance

A natural green valley, watered by two sparkling, life-giving springs was a welcome stopping place for the overland travelers going through the area. This valley was settled in 1855 by thirty men sent by Brigham Young, then Governor of the territory, to build a fort and stockade there. The fort was abandoned in 1857.

Today that once quiet valley is one of the great entertainment centers of the world and Nevada's largest, fastest-growing city — Las Vegas.

The most expensive entertainers of the world receive their largest fees for keeping Las Vegas' visitors amused. Casinos, night clubs, the most elegant hotels — all are designed to coax ever more visitors.

The modern history of Las Vegas began with a railroad tent town in 1905. Less than sixty years later, that tent town could boast one of the largest and most expensive "tents" anywhere. This is the huge new multi-million dollar convention center, seating 8,000 people and providing for conventions with as many as 30,000 in attendance.

Las Vegas is also a city of homes, a city where there are more churches per person than anywhere else in the country.

Las Vegas is a handy center for visiting many nearby areas of interest. Mt. Charleston offers mountain recreation in the midst of the desert. Lake Mead and both rims of Grand Canyon are easy drives from Las Vegas.

Government installations near Las Vegas include the U. S. Air Force Bombing and Gunnery School and the atomic testing ground.

Biggest celebration in this continually celebrating city is the annual Helldorado. Everyone jumps into early-day western garb and tries to turn the clock back to olden days. No one seems to care very much that this is just about the only place in Nevada which was not a wild mining town. The past in Las Vegas was not nearly so rip-roaring as the present.

Instant Facts

Became 36th state October 31, 1864
Capital — Carson City
State Flower — Sagebrush
State Tree — Piñon Pine
State Song — *Home Means Nevada*
State Motto — *All for Our Country*
Area — 110,690 square miles
Greatest Length (north to south) — 484 miles
Greatest Width (east to west) — 316 miles
Highest Point — 13,145 feet
Lowest Point — 470 feet
Population — 285,000 (1960)
Highest recorded temperature — 122°
Lowest recorded temperature — minus 50°
Population Density — 2.6 persons per square mile (1960 census)

Principal Cities —		
Las Vegas	64,400	(1960)
Reno	51,470	
North Las Vegas	18,422	
Sparks	16,618	
Henderson	12,525	
Elko	6,298	
Carson City	5,163	

You Have a Date With History

1826 Explorations of Peter Skene Ogden
1829 Birth of Dat-So-La-Lee
1833 Expedition of Joseph Walker
1843 Explorations of Fremont and Kit Carson
1848 Nevada becomes United States territory
1849 Mormon Station (Genoa) first permanent settlement
1850 Utah Territory (including Nevada) formed.
1858 Carson City founded
1859 Comstock boom begins
1861 Nevada Territory created
1864 Nevada attains statehood
1868 Continental Railroad crosses Nevada
1871 State Capitol Building completed
1874 University of Nevada established at Elko, moved to Reno 1885.
1897 Corbett-Fitzsimmons championship, Carson City
1906 Tonopah boom at peak
1915 Lahontan Dam constructed
1931 Gambling made legal
1936 Hoover Dam completed
1951 Establishment of Nevada Proving Ground, Atomic Energy Com.
1959 Boulder City transferred from federal to state control
1963 Atmospherium-Planetarium opened at Reno

Thinkers, Doers, Fighters

People of renown who have been associated with Nevada

Clemens, Samuel (Mark Twain)
Dat-So-La-Lee
Fair, James
Flood, James
Goodman, Joseph
Harrington, Mark
Hearst, George
Mackay, John
Mordy, Wendell A.
Nye, James Warren
O'Brien, William
Scrugham, James G.
Stewart, William Morris
Thompson, John A.
Wilson, Jack
Winnemucca
Wixon, Emma
Wright, William (Dan De Quille)

Governors of Nevada

H. G. Blasdel (1864-1870)
L. R. Bradley (1871-1878)
John H. Kinkead (1879-1882)
Jewett W. Adams (1883-1886)
C. C. Stevenson (1887-1890)
Frank Bell (1890)
R. K. Colcord (1891-1894)
John E. Jones (1895-1896)
Reinhold Sadler (1898-1902)
John Sparks (1903-1908)
Denver S. Dickerson (1908-1910)
Tasker L. Oddie (1911-1914)
Emmet D. Boyle (1915-1922)
James G. Scrugham (1923-1926)
Fred B. Balzar (1927-1934)
Morley Griswold (1934)
Richard Kirman, Sr. (1935-1938)
E. P. Carville (1939-1945)
Vail M. Pittman (1946)
Charles H. Russell (1951-1958)
Grant Sawyer (1958-   )

Annual Events

May — Helldorado, Las Vegas
May — Five State Sports Car Jamboree, Winnemucca
June — Reno Rodeo
June — Stampede at Elko
August — Pony Express Days, Ely
September — Nevada Rodeo, Winnemucca
September — Races, Elko
September — Community Fair, Las Vegas
October — Sahara Cup Races, Lake Mead
October — Nevada Day, Carson City

INDEX